Charge into Reading

Decodable Reader
with literacy activities

Hop, Frog!
Short O

Brooke Vitale • Katarzyna Jasinska

CHARGE MOMMY
BOOKS
Riverside, CT

Copyright © 2022 Charge Mommy Books, LLC. All rights reserved.

No part of this book may be reproduced or transmitted in any form or by any means, electronic or mechanical, including photocopying, recording, or by any information storage and retrieval system, without written permission from the publisher.

For information address contact@chargemommybooks.com
or visit chargemommybooks.com.

Printed in China
ISBN: 978-1-955947-20-6
10 9 8 7

Designed by Lindsay Broderick
Created in consultation with literacy specialist Marisa Ware, MSEd

Publisher's Cataloging-in-Publication Data
Names: Vitale, Brooke, author. | Jasinska, Katarzyna, illustrator.
Title: Hop, frog! : short o decodable reader / Brooke Vitale, Katarzyna Jasinska.
Description: Riverside, CT : Charge Mommy Books, 2022.| Illustrated early reader. | Series: Charge into Reading. | Audience: Ages 4-6. | Summary: Introduces children to the short O sound. Includes eight pages of short O literacy activities at the end.
Identifiers: LCCN 2022901735 | ISBN 9781955947206 (pbk.)
Subjects: LCSH: Frogs -- Juvenile fiction. | Reading -- Code emphasis approaches -- Juvenile literature. | Reading -- Phonetic method -- Juvenile literature. | Readers (Primary). | BISAC: JUVENILE FICTION / Animals / Frogs & Toads. | JUVENILE FICTION / Readers / Beginner. | JUVENILE FICTION / Concepts / Sounds.
Classification: LCC PZ7.1 V59 Hop 2022 | DDC E V59ho--dc22
LC record available at https://lccn.loc.gov/2022901735

Tod is a frog.
Tod is hot.

Tod spots a dock.

Tod hops.
Hop, hop, hop.

Tod hops on the dock.
The dock is hot!

Tod hops off.

Tod spots a rock.

Tod hops on the rock.
The rock is hot!

Tod hops off.

Tod is lost.
Hop, Tod, hop!

Tod spots a log.

Tod hops on top.

Stop!
Tod spots a pond.

Plop!

The pond is not hot.
Tod is not hot!

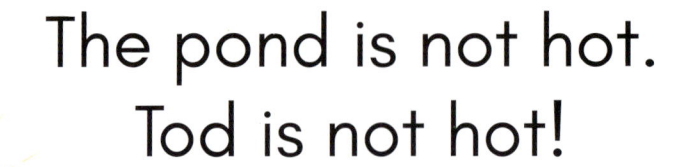

Let's Talk Literacy!

Read the sentence below. Then circle the picture that matches the sentence.

Tod hops on a log.

Let's Talk Literacy!

Say the name of each picture below. As you speak, **tap out** the sounds for each word. Then **write the letter(s)** for each sound in the box.

Answers: f-o-x/f-r-o-g/r-o-ck

Let's Talk Literacy!

Say the name of each picture below. Then circle the words that make a **short O sound**.

Answers: dot, log, rock, box

Let's Talk Literacy!

Say the name of the picture in each row. Then circle the word in each row that is part of the same **word family**.

dog

pod log con got mob

pot

bop mom dog not rod

fox

lob sob lox nod fog

Let's Talk Literacy!

Say the word. Then look at the picture to figure out its **rhyming word**. Change the first letter of the word to make the new word, and write it on the line.

Word	Change to	New word
log	(cog)	_____
top	(mop)	_____
dock	(lock)	_____

Let's Talk Literacy!

Look at each picture below. Then read the words below each picture. **Circle the word** that matches the picture.

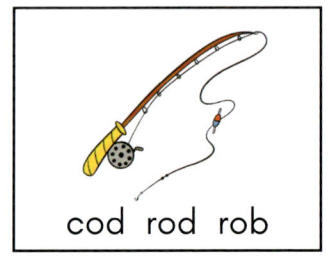

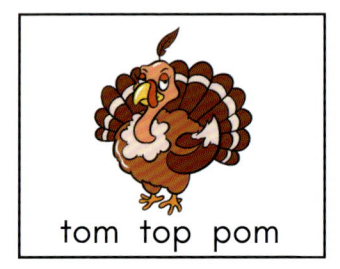

dock lock log	pot pod top	log frog lob
cob cop mop	cod rod rob	tom top pom

Let's Talk Literacy!

The word **bog** is part of the **-OG word family**. Name the pictures below. Then circle the ones that are also part of the -OG word family.

Answers: cog, frog, log, dog

Let's Talk Literacy!

Say the name of each picture below. Then draw a line to the letter that makes the **first sound** in the word.

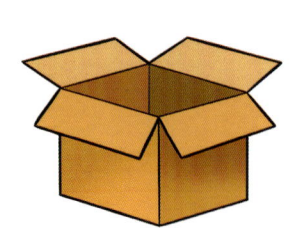

Mm   Bb   Tt   Pp   Ll   Ff